THE

Book Itch

Is There a Book In You?

THE

Book Itch
Is There a Book In You?

How to *Leave Your Legacy* to the World

ADAM WITTY   ALLEN FAHDEN

Published by Advantage, Charleston, South Carolina.
Member of Advantage Media Group.

ADVANTAGE is a registered trademark and the Advantage colophon is a trademark of Advantage Media Group, Inc.

Printed in the United States of America.

ISBN: 978-159932-362-6
LCCN: 2012956015

This publication is designed to provide accurate and authoritative information in regard to the subject matter covered. It is sold with the understanding that the publisher is not engaged in rendering legal, accounting, or other professional services. If legal advice or other expert assistance is required, the services of a competent professional person should be sought.

Advantage Media Group is proud to be a part of the Tree Neutral® program. Tree Neutral offsets the number of trees consumed in the production and printing of this book by taking proactive steps such as planting trees in direct proportion to the number of trees used to print books. To learn more about Tree Neutral, please visit **www.treeneutral.com**. To learn more about Advantage's commitment to being a responsible steward of the environment, please visit **www.advantagefamily.com/green**

Advantage Media Group is a publisher of business, self-improvement, and professional development books and online learning. We help entrepreneurs, business leaders, and professionals share their Stories, Passion, and Knowledge to help others Learn & Grow™. Do you have a manuscript or book idea that you would like us to consider for publishing? Please visit advantagefamily.com or call 1.866.775.1696.

This book is dedicated to the entrepreneurs, business leaders, and professionals that have Stories, Passion, and Knowledge to share with the world.

Table of Contents

Table of Contents

REGISTER
YOUR BOOK

AND ACCESS FREE RESOURCES FOR POTENTIAL AUTHORS!

It doesn't matter where you are in the world, Adam and Al can help you share your Stories, Passion, and Knowledge with the world in the form of a published book.

Visit THEBOOKITCH.COM to access these free resources:

 REQUEST a complimentary copy of Adam Witty's best-selling book *21 Ways to Build Your Business with a Book: Secrets to Dramatically Grow Your Income, Credibility, and Celebrity-Power by Being an Author* while supplies last

 RECEIVE a subscription to the Author Success University™ and Insights with Experts™ monthly teleseminars wherein successful authors and book marketing experts reveal their tips and tricks for marketing and growing a business with a book

 REGISTER for a webinar led by Adam Witty: "How to Quickly Write, Publish, And Profit From A Book That Will Explode Your Business"

 COMPLETE Advantage's Publishing Questionnaire and receive a complimentary Discovery Call with an acquisitions editor to help you determine if your ideas, concepts, or manuscript are worth turning into a book

ACCESS ALL OF THE ABOVE FREE RESOURCES
BY REGISTERING YOUR BOOK AT
THEBOOKITCH.COM/REGISTER

THE BURNING YEARNING.
WILL IT MATTER THAT
YOU WERE HERE?

In the beginning you had a dream.

Remember? You were going to change the world. You were itching to make your mark.

You had a dream.

Do you still?

Look inside. The dream, that passion to make the world a better place, is still there, isn't it? Maybe you think about all the wisdom you've gained, the lessons you've learned. How can you pass this knowledge on to others?

DO YOU OFTEN WONDER HOW TO LEAVE YOUR MARK ON THE WORLD?

Can you reach down, past all the disappointments and all the sweet victories, and touch the deep ache inside of you that drives you onward, no matter what the difficulty? Can you tap that determined spirit that makes you get up again and again, no matter how many times you get knocked down?

That desire is still in you.

But now it means more. You have learned so much along the way.

You no longer long to leave your mark on the world: you need to create your legacy to give the world.

Not one of us knows how much time we have left on this earth. If you want to leave your mark, now is the time to do it.

THERE ARE SEVERAL WAYS TO LEAVE YOUR MARK.

UNFORTUNATELY, FEW ARE LEGAL.

AND EVEN FEWER LAST.

There's something that only you can give to the world. You need to share it in a way the world will hear it and celebrate it.

To make a difference, you must be different. Why? With the constant bombardment of information, especially through the Internet and television, you need to stand out and above the crowd.

"The volume of global information doubles every two years," reports Richard Bennison, Chief Operating Officer of the global business consulting firm, KPMG. "By 2020, the world will generate 50 times the amount of information we do today. The world has never been more connected. In three years' time, 91 percent of the world's population will own a mobile phone."

The world is plugged in to an amazing source for communicating with each other. The world is listening, waiting for wisdom and hope.

Seize the chance to send your call to every one of them.

THIS IS NOT A BOOK ABOUT WHY YOU SHOULD WRITE A BOOK.

IT'S ABOUT WHETHER YOU SHOULD WRITE A BOOK.

Writing a book can be one of the stupidest things you've ever done. The average book sells less than 200 copies. And now with the 170 percent yearly growth of eBooks, not even the cost of printing can keep all the bozos out of the game.

The task of creating a book isn't pretty. If you write a book, you may have to deal with writer's block. You will have to

determine which insights and experiences will fascinate people, and which ones will make them drop the book as they nod off to sleep. While organizing your knowledge, you can get lost in the trivial details. Once you turn your book over to an editor, having someone nitpicking your grammar and writing skills may insult you. Becoming an author is a murky path full of self-questioning and isolation.

But if you can get to the finish line, a well-conceived book can catapult you to stardom faster than Kim Kardashian after her sex tape was leaked.

2

DO YOU ITCH?
CAN YOU SCRATCH?

Most people start writing their book way before they're ready, and without knowing whether or not their motivation will carry them through.

As a result, they put hours and hours into their book, only to realize later on that they've been writing the same chapter over and over again.

"How's the book coming?"

"I'm on page 800."

"When are you going to finish?"

"I don't know. At page 180, I thought it
would be a 300 page book."

"What happened?

"The book
took over.
And it won't
let me stop."

**IF YOU DON'T KNOW
WHERE YOU'RE GOING,**

**HOW WILL YOU KNOW
WHEN YOU GET THERE?**

Too many books travel far yet go nowhere.

That's because the writers started writing
before they started thinking.

Sometimes, you start out excited about your book, only to find out nobody else cares what you're writing about.

Other times, you write yourself into a corner, feeling like you've run out of things to say long before you run out of space to fill.

Painful questions begin to plague you:

Where is this book going?

Did somebody already write this book?

Can I put together a coherent sentence?

If you don't want your book writing experience to feel like a remake of Stephen King's *The Shining,* take the Author Score quiz (THEBOOKITCH.COM) and find out whether writing a book is right for you. Just take it *before* you start writing. After all, all work and no play makes Jack a dull boy.

CUT DOWN THE AUTHOR/BOOK DIVORCE RATE.

Everybody's writing a book. It's just that nobody's finishing a book. Instead, somewhere along the way, almost every would-be author, disillusioned, files for divorce from the book.

I never thought it would: (Insert reason here or choose from the following)

Take this much time.

Be so frustrating.

Make me feel lost.

AUTHOR SCORE QUIZ MEASURES ASPECTS FOR WRITING A BOOK THAT MOST HAVEN'T CONSIDERED.

Take the Author Score quiz and make a more informed decision about whether a book is right for you. This measures two aspects for writing a book that most people haven't considered.

The Itch Score answers the question: Are you motivated?

The Scratch Score answers the question: Are you ready?

WHY MARRY YOUR BOOK?
INSTEAD, SPEED-DATE IT.

Just go to THEBOOKITCH.COM.
Once you take this 3-minute online quiz,
you will get two scores: a motivation score
and a readiness score.

Your Itch Motivation
Score comes from
outside the con-
text of a book. It
allows you to see
how your reasons
for writing a book
in the first place will
sustain you throughout the
process, no matter what happens.

Your Scratch Readiness Score comes from
inside the context of the book. It will help
you to work on the value and uniqueness

of your message, to make sure it is unique and clearly expressed. This is an iterative process that will take longer than you think, but will contribute the majority of the value to your book.

HAVE YOUR BOOK GO SWIMMINGLY, INSTEAD OF DROWNING.

When you're writing a book, actually writing the book is one of the last things you are doing. In Chapter 10, we will show you how to get ready to write your book, so you can scratch the book itch successfully.

Here's the bonus: The more ready you are, the less motivation it requires to get you through the process.

Just go to THEBOOKITCH.COM and follow the prompts.

3

ZOOM OUT FOR MOTIVATION AND SIGNIFICANCE

Can you find your passion when it doesn't seem to be there?

When Charles Revson was the CEO of Revlon, a reporter asked him how he liked the cosmetics business.

"I'm not in the cosmetics business," replied Revson. "I sell hope."

When you look at your own business or what you do in that business from a higher level, you'll see things quite differently. To see things differently, go back to when you first started out. Were you happy just to have a job, or were you on a mission?

Sadly, research says that most people who start businesses do so to replicate the job they just left. Same job, no boss. (That's most likely not you. If it was, you wouldn't be anywhere near this book.)

Even then, you saw a world that needed what you had: a world ready for you to make your presence known. Now, with all this experience behind you, can you remember what it's really about?

"Try to convince a fish of the concept of water."

Marshall MacLuhan

To be an expert, you need to remember what it is like to be a beginner. When we excel at something, that also means we know too much. We can no longer see some of the things we used to see, when our eyes were more innocent. That can make it tough to explain our knowledge to a beginner. So, let's zoom out, and get you to a different perch.

If you were in the cosmetics business, how would you go from selling lipstick to selling hope?

ZOOM OUT BY ASKING THE "ADVANTAGE" QUESTIONS:

Q: What's the advantage of lipstick?

A: It makes your face look better.

Q: What's the advantage of making your face look better?

A: It attracts more people to you.

Q: What's the advantage of attracting more people to you?

A: It gives you a better hope of having love in your life.

"People don't want quarter inch drills. They want quarter inch holes."

Leo McGinneva

You can get to the same place by zooming out of quarter inch drills. Again, ask the "advantage" questions:

Q: What's the advantage of quarter inch drills?

A: They put holes in the wall.

A drill is a product or feature. A hole is the benefit the drill gives the buyer. People don't need to have a drill lying around the house.

They want a hole in the wall. The drill will give them the end result they desire.

Now you try. Start with your book. What's it about? What's the message? Let's say your book is about getting people to work in their strengths.

Q: What's the advantage of getting people to work in their strengths?

A. They do better work, faster.

Q: What's the advantage of doing better work, faster?

A: They produce more.

Q: What's the advantage of people producing more?

A: They make the business more valuable.

Q: What's the advantage of making the business more valuable?

A: You get rich and maybe even famous.

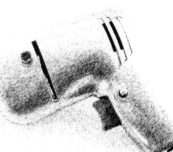

IT'S NOT THE DRILL OR THE HOLE; IT'S THE ABILITY TO PUT A HOLE IN THE WALL WITH NO DUST FROM THE SHEET ROCK.

Now review your answers. Ask yourself, "Which of these create the most value for my reader?" Then ask your potential readers, "Which is most important to you?"

OFTEN, THE MOST POWERFUL PART OF YOUR MESSAGE LIES BETWEEN THE FEATURE AND THE BENEFIT. IT'S CALLED THE *ADVANTAGE*.

It's not the drill or the hole; it's the ability to put a hole in the wall with no dust from the sheet rock. It's not the lipstick or the hope; it's the ability to draw attention to the right parts of your face, which leads to compliments and attracting the people you want to meet.

Once you find the advantage—the most powerful part of your message—put it everywhere in your book. But don't forget the feature and the benefit; you'll use those to help prove your case for delivering the advantage.

BUILD YOUR BUSINESS
WITH A BOOK

If you have nothing that sets you apart, then you're a commodity, just like all the other nobodies who are trying to get the same business that you want. But if you're an author, the credibility machine starts up all by itself.

NO ONE EVER SPENT FOUR HOURS ON AN AIRPLANE READING YOUR BUSINESS CARD.

Your book does everything you could ever do in person, and a lot more. Through your book, someone who has never heard of you is compelled to get to know you and how you think. Through your words and ideas, your book establishes you as an authority on something that's important to the reader. If you think the words "pleased to meet you" sound good, imagine the words, "I just finished reading your book."

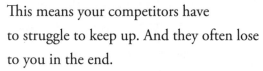

IS IT A LEVEL PLAYING FIELD? NO. IT'S TILTED IN YOUR FAVOR.

When you have a compelling and original book in your area of expertise, you make the rules of the game. This means your competitors have to struggle to keep up. And they often lose to you in the end.

What's more, your book propels you ahead in another way. When you meet a prospect who has read even part of your book, they're already convinced of your point of view. You go from being an unwanted pest to a welcomed guest. This can save you days and weeks of selling to the wrong people, at the wrong time.

After all, how hard is it to respond to a request for a proposal when it's written for you?

THE BOOK ITCH. SHOULD YOU SCRATCH IT?

In a recent study by RainToday, the premier online source for growing your business, authors reported that writing and publishing a book made a huge difference in their *visibility, income, and business success.*

➚ *96 percent said having a book positively influenced their business.*

➚ *96 percent generated more clients.*

➚ *94 percent generated more leads.*

➚ *87 percent charged higher fees.*

↗ *87 percent attracted a more desirable client base.*

↗ *76 percent closed more deals.*

1. VISIBILITY: BE FAMOUS

- A book gives you a 30,000-word business card.

- A book makes you dramatically different.

- A book gets you heard above the noise.

- A book allows you to compete with titans and giants.

- A book gets you recognized for your authority and expertise.

- A book gives you the ultimate networking tool.

- A book builds brand recognition and equity for your company.

2. INCOME: BE PROSPEROUS

- A book creates client loyalty.

- A book generates quality referrals.

- A book gives you an income stream.

- A book generates leads.

- A book gives you greater credibility.

- A book makes you a highly paid, sought after speaker.

- A book becomes a profitable ancillary product.

3. SUCCESS: BE EVERYWHERE

- A book puts you in multiple places at once.

- A book gives you a cost-effective marketing tool.

- A book spreads your message worldwide.

- A book builds employee loyalty and provides employee training.

- A book increases sales without salespeople.

- A book makes you a darling of the media and gets you free publicity and media coverage.

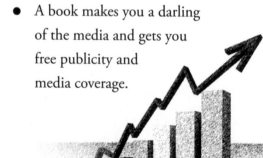

(Radio shows alone interview 10,000 people every day, many of whom are authors. What reason have you given them to want to talk to you?)

GOOD THINGS HAPPEN TO PEOPLE WHO WRITE THE RIGHT BOOK.

Nobody had ever heard of Tim Ferris until he wrote *The Four-Hour Work Week* and promoted it uniquely on the Internet. Now he's a business guru and commands tens of thousands of dollars for a speech.

If you get to the other side of writing and completing your book, you become one of a select few. So maybe, just maybe, it's worth what a pain in the ass it is to get there.

YOUR BOOK LIVES LONG
AFTER YOU DO

When you focus on the part of your message with the most *advantage*, amazing things begin to happen. Not only do the people in your audience understand you, they "get" you. This means that they take on part of your message as their own, which then leads them to spread it to others.

WHY WRITE A BOOK? BECAUSE YOU JUST MIGHT START A MOVEMENT.

Imagine thousands of people spreading your message. This is the kind of legacy that takes on its own life.

1. Steve Jobs is gone, but his philosophy continues to inspire innovation, beauty and simplicity.

2. Dr. Edwards Deming passed, but his quality movement lives on.

3. Napoleon Hill died 40 years ago, but his book, *Think and Grow Rich*, is amazingly still #331 on Amazon, out of six million books.

WHAT WILL CONTINUE
AFTER YOU'RE GONE?

If the motivation part of your Author Score quiz says you're not motivated enough to get through the lengthy process of creating your book, you need something that will make you get up every time you're knocked down.

Ask yourself these questions:

1. Will my life have mattered?

2. What will people be able to do as a result of my thinking?

3. What about my work will continue because someone else is inspired to take it to the next level?

4. What will people thank me for?

5. What problems will go away
   when people do what I suggest?

HERE'S HOW TO FIND OUT
WHAT'S IMPORTANT TO YOU.

First, get out of the past *and* get out of the present.

The reptilian part of the brain tends to remember all the slights, the embarrassments and even the humiliations. It does this because it wants to keep these events from repeating.

**HOW MUCH CAN YOU MILK
BEING "SCISSOR MONITOR"
IN FIFTH GRADE?**

Why would
you want to
be in the past anyway?
Remembering the times
you felt like a geek in high school
will not help you put out a great book.
Neither will thinking about the time you
threw up in what's her name's car. Not
even the positive things will help. After
all, how much can you milk being "scissor
monitor" in fifth grade?

Go to the future. Not the future in your
fears, but the future of your dreams. Ask
this question: "If I were to write a book
and the outcome was ideal, what would
happen?"

Go to the point in the future where this would happen, and speak about it in the present tense. First, what would ideally happen for you?

- I am in the top five on the *New York Times* bestseller list.

- I am the keynote speaker at 25 major conferences.

- I have appeared on all the major television networks.

- My website gets five million hits a month.

- I've been on Letterman three times.

Then, what would ideally happen for others? Envision the outcome caused by the specific advantages presented in your book.

- People routinely say how my work has changed their lives.

- My book launched thousands of new businesses.

- People who practice my methods perform 30 percent more efficiently in their work.

- Cancer survivors now live an extra five years.

- People now tell others how much they care.

Once you realize what's important about what you're doing, and what's possible for yourself and others as a result, you can use it to keep yourself going and break through the walls that will inevitably appear.

NO ONE CAN MISQUOTE YOU IN YOUR OWN BOOK.

Let's say your book takes off, and you are faced with a new set of de-motivators:

- What if I'm misunderstood?

- What if people say bad things about me?

- What if someone does something bad, then blames me?

These are fears everyone has when they step into a public arena. Yet, you have a great built-in protection from just about everything you fear.

"I don't care what you say about me. Just spell my name right."

-Most often attributed to P.T. Barnum

In our culture, celebrity trumps everything. Ask Donald Trump. He's been back from failure many times.

Before she wrote the Harry Potter series, billionaire J.K. Rowling was a severely depressed mother with no source of income and no future.

Oprah Winfrey was fired from her first job and called "unfit for TV."

Walt Disney lost his first newspaper job after his editor said, "you'll never have any creative ideas."

When you write your book, it immortalizes your stories, passion, and knowledge. You become the authority on the subject, and it matters little what your detractors say, unless, of course, they misspell your name.

6

CAN YOU GET IT FINISHED?

Now that you are motivated and ready to write your book, you have one final barrier: Does creating a book fit your core strengths?

Why is this important? Some people are natural starters and some are natural finishers. Some prefer to think, some prefer to act. Put these together and you have a different way of looking at your ability to create and complete the book that you want.

Natural starters do well at the beginning of a project when the direction has not yet been set, things are up for grabs and ideas are still in play. Then, as the project gets more and more set, the starters tend to get bored and move on to other projects.

Natural finishers do well after the direction has been set. They can focus on taking care of the details without worrying about what can go wrong. They are uncomfortable at the beginning of the project, because they see so many things that could endanger the project.

Natural thinkers focus on strategy and what decisions need to be made. Their strength is to make sure you have a well conceived and thoroughly thought-out idea. Often, this is at the cost of ignoring the action they need to take. Many thinkers will walk out of the room after they've made the decision, hoping that things will magically get done.

Natural doers focus on tactics and what plan needs to be designed and implemented. Their strength is to get into action and help things get done quickly. Without the thinkers, the doers will take action on items and, at worst, get a lot of mean-ingless tasks done.

NATURAL THINKERS FOCUS ON STRATEGY AND WHAT DECISIONS NEED TO BE MADE.

YOU CAN MAKE YOUR BOOK PROJECT EASIER, BETTER AND FASTER.

HAND IT OFF FROM STRENGTH TO STRENGTH.

Take the Author Score quiz to see where you fit in the process and identify who should be on your team. Then, use a process based on getting the right parts of the work to the right strength at the right time. Actual work tests show that a project goes three to eight times faster when handed off from strength to strength.

A PROJECT GOES THREE TO EIGHT TIMES FASTER WHEN HANDED OFF FROM STRENGTH TO STRENGTH.

I's (IDEA people, starters and thinkers) work best when solving problems and thinking of ideas to make you stand out from the crowd. These people can help you make your book different so it will be noticed and sell well.

T's (TACTICS people, starters and doers) work best when setting priorities and planning the launch of your best ideas, so you can use your resources on what will produce the most results. Tactics people help you know what to do next.

C's (CHALLENGE people, finishers and thinkers) work best when warning you about what can go wrong and critiquing your plan. Challenge people make sure you're not blind-sided by problems you didn't anticipate. They help you bullet proof your case. They also keep you organized.

H's (HANDS-ON people, finishers and doers) work best when handling the details. They don't even want to be in the meeting when you're planning your book. Just let them take care of the finishing touches. These people can execute the line edit and carry out the details to perfection.

Once you take the Author Score quiz, you will learn three important skills:

1. How to choose a role in your book project that energizes you rather than drains you.

2. How to recruit people with different strengths than yours, so you have the highest performing team possible.

3. How to use a process that gets the right parts of the work, to the right strengths, at the right time, for speed and quality.

This will make your book fun, instead of a nightmare. You won't lose your message and get overwhelmed by all the moving parts. If you use everyone's strengths well, the end result will be a high quality read that shines above all of the other books on the subject.

Just go to THEBOOKITCH.COM and find out how to make your book project so much easier and more rewarding.

7

RIGHT ROLE,
RIGHT TEAMMATES

If you're getting the idea from the Author Score quiz that people are different, you're right. In fact, people are so different that the whole idea of a team has become a paradox.

Research shows that the highest performing teams combine people of different strengths. But, research also shows that when you combine all these different strengths, you increase the chance of conflict.

Thus the paradox: the more diverse your team is for high performance, the more potential conflict can hinder high performance.

Is throw out ideas and **C**s shoot them down. **T**s propose actions and **H**s tell them they're moving too fast on ideas that make no sense.

Then, after that, it can get even worse, which sends your book ahead on a road to nowhere.

WHEN YOU COMBINE DIFFERENT STRENGTHS, YOU INCREASE THE CHANCE OF CONFLICT.

HOW TO BEAT THE DIVERSE TEAM PARADOX? IT'S ALL IN THE HANDOFFS.

The Author Score quiz will help you get all of the right people in the right place, where they can contribute the most, with the least amount of unproductive conflict.

When you create your book, you'll zoom through the parts you're good at and wallow in the parts you hate. That's why there's a particular strength and a resulting role for every part of the process. Together, they spell **I.T.C.H.** Using people's **I.T.C.H.** strengths will help you scratch the book itch.

THE "I" STRENGTH IS FOR IDEAS.

If your highest score is starting and thinking combined, you're an **I**. This means you should create the concept of the book. You should generate the ideas about:

- What makes the book different?

- What are the underlying principles of the book?

- What is the outline for the book?

You should then hand your work off to the **T**.

THE "T" STRENGTH IS FOR TACTICS.

If your highest score is starting and doing combined, you're a **T**. This means you should establish the plan and priorities for

the book. You choose the best ideas from
the **I** and design a launch plan that covers:

- Who is the audience?

- Where are they?

- How do we best reach them?

You should then hand your work off to
the **C**.

THE "C" STRENGTH IS
FOR CHALLENGES.

If your highest score is
finishing and thinking
combined, you're a **C**.
This means you should identify
the challenges and organize the
content for the book. You critique the
plans from the **T** and raise all the issues
about what can go wrong:

IDENTIFY CHALLENGES AND
ORGANIZE THE CONTENT
OF YOUR BOOK.

- What needs to be backed
  up by studies?

- If someone pushes back, what
  will they most likely say?

- How could this information be
  better organized for clarity?

You should then hand the work off back
to the *I* to generate ideas on how to over-
come the challenges. The *T* then picks the

best ideas and the **C** phases them into the plan. Next, the **I** creates an outline, the **T** makes sure it's in the right order and writes the first draft of the manuscript. The **T** turns this over to the **C** for a rough edit, and then to the **H** for the final edit.

THE "H" STRENGTH IS FOR HANDS-ON.

If your highest score is finishing and doing combined, you're an **H**. This means you should take care of the details for the book. You take the rough, edited manuscript from the **C**, and dot all the i's and cross all the t's. In your final edit, you make sure there are no errors and the details conform to the elements of style and other protocols for a beautifully finished book. You take care of:

- The line edit.

- Conforming to the rules of publishing.

- The details that make reading the book a great experience.

If you can get your team working on the parts they do best, then handing off your book strength to strength, you get it all done much faster, way better and even cheaper. Plus it's a lot more fun and satisfying. After all, when you scratch the book itch, it should feel really good.

THE "H" STRENGTH IS FOR HANDS ON.

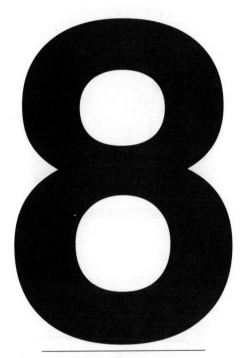

8

WRITE THE RIGHT BOOK BEFORE YOU START WRITING

THE SMARTER YOU START, THE BETTER YOU FINISH.

As mentioned earlier, the average book sells less than 200 copies. After years of packaging and promoting books in attention-getting ways, we see authors make the same common mistakes over and over.

By the time they think about what should happen before they produce the book, it's usually too late. They wrote the book. They named it. They designed the cover. They printed it.

Writers can be so passionate about their subjects that it's hard to focus on the needs of the reader. They are often so close to their work that they can't identify which parts of their message others hunger to hear. Without this understanding, books often fail to highlight the most appealing, saleable parts of the message.

HOW TO AVOID THE PAIN OF WRITING THE WRONG BOOK: THE BOOK RIGHTER

Address the four major factors that result in book sales:

1. The Right Audience

When most people think of their target audience they consider age and income.

These factors do not lead to book sales. Instead, focus on the aspects of your target audience that pinpoint readers' motivation to buy your book.

Key Distinction: Your message needs to excel at all three aspects of marketing effectiveness:

> Dramatic difference +
> overt benefit +
> reason to believe
>
> ───────────────────
>
> = do all three well and
> get 240 times the results

In *Jumpstart Your Marketing Brain*, Doug Hall proved extraordinary results come from being different. In a meta study of over 900 marketing journal studies, he pointed out that if you do three things well, you get 240 times the result. The three concepts are dramatic difference, overt benefit and reason to believe. Of the three, dramatic difference alone accounts for more than 50 percent of the results.

When you analyze your message, ask yourself:

1. How is my message different than that of any other book written on the subject?

2. How is my message obviously beneficial to the reader? Am I burying the benefit to the reader in my own story or interest in myself?

3. How can I lay out a strong
    case for why my message is
    believable and important?

4. What problem do I solve?

5. What irritations come
    with the problem?

6. What other attempts to solve this
    problem have failed and why?

7. Have other books
    on my topic soured
    the category?

2. The Right Emotions

Virtually every marketing study shows
that emotions drive buying behavior.
That's why you should identify the feelings, both positive and negative, that you

can address during the four parts of the
buying process.

Capitalize on negative feelings about
the reader's current situation. People are
motivated to avoid pain and seek pleasure.
However, they are *more* motivated to *avoid*
pain than to *seek* pleasure. So, begin by
identifying what pain people wish to avoid
and how your message helps them avoid it.

Associate your book with positive feelings
about the solution. Head off negative
feelings that could upset
people about your mes-
sage. The easiest way to
do this is to directly
address the

negative comments that your potential challengers will make when they read or hear about your book.

3. The Right Message

Is your message unique? How can you make it more unique and powerful? Who are your chief competitors and how are you different? How do you appear to be different enough to get the attention you need, without the most predictable problems associated with unique messages?

4. The Right Pieces at the Right Time

Most authors start thinking about marketing after the horse is already out of the barn. At the start they ask: "What do I have to say?" Then they write their book.

Instead, ask: "What do I have to say that is different enough that someone will spend money to read it?" This way you'll get the answers early in your book process, while you still have time to do it right.

If you are not different, then you are a commodity. This means people will only buy your offering at the lowest possible price. If you are different, you play in uncontested market space.

IF YOU ARE DIFFERENT, YOU PLAY IN UNCONTESTED MARKET SPACE.

Renee Mauborgne and W. Chan Kim lay out the importance of being different in everything you offer in their enlightening book, *Blue Ocean Strategy.* Only 14 percent of the companies they studied play in uncontested market space. They get 38 percent of the revenue and 61 percent of the profit.

Analyze and adapt your message to the three parameters *before* you start writing. When you figure out how to make your book solve buyers' pain before you write it, you can avoid your own pain—of realizing what your book should have said, when it is too late or too expensive to make changes.

FIGURE OUT HOW TO MAKE YOUR BOOK SOLVE BUYERS' PAIN BEFORE YOU WRITE IT.

WHAT TO FOCUS ON TO HELP YOU WRITE THE RIGHT BOOK:

Uniquely Identify Target Audiences:

- Un-met Needs (Example: a book on weight loss. How to take it in tiny steps so you can get through to the other end of the program.)

- Driving Emotions (Example: Frustration with programs that don't work, and shame about being overweight.)

- Irritations with Present Alternatives (Example: Thousands of programs that promise big results for little effort, most of which are untrue.)

CREATE MEANINGFUL DIFFERENTIATION:

- Competitive Analysis (Example: People who pretend to do what you do.)

- Important Issues Where They Are Weak (Example: Having an original thought.)

- Solutions to Their Weaknesses (Example: You having original thoughts.)

GENERATE UNIQUE CONCEPTS AND TEST THEM. WHAT IS IT THAT MAKES YOUR BOOK DIFFERENT?:

- Visuals for Testing

- Titles for Testing

- Publicity Ideas

- Arresting Cover Visuals

- High-Readership Headlines

- Compelling Cover Copy

- Statements for Testing

- Memorable
  Internet
  Domain
  Names

> IF PEOPLE YOU ARE NOT CLOSE TO HAVE A VISCERAL REACTION, YOU HAVE A POWERFUL IDEA.

IDENTIFY BUSINESS OPPORTUNITIES AND TEST THEM:

- Follow-up on
  Product Concepts

- Ideas for Vertical
  Market Sales

- Elevator Pitch—
  This is your "I don't sell cosmetics,
  I sell hope" message; short enough
  to motivate a CEO on an elevator.

When you test concepts on people, select people you are *not* close to. If they have a visceral reaction, you have a powerful idea. You can test for two things: clarity and taste. Clarity is easy. Just ask, "What do you get out of this?" If they respond the way you intend—you win. If not, make it more obvious. Taste can cause you much more grief. To be powerful and warrant attention, big ideas often border on bad taste. You don't want to offend your market. But then again, you can offend them by boring them.

These will put you way ahead of the competition, because today most people jump into the tactics of their marketing without much for strategy. Read these books and you can craft a strategy that will make you different enough to stand out, and compelling enough to make the sale.

9

WILL SCRATCHING
PAY OFF?

Imagine a day that begins with deciding
what you're going to do. It's a day when
no one owns your time but you. Even if
you do nothing that day, your income will
continue to come in. As you linger over
the newspaper in your favorite coffee shop,
someone you don't know asks what you do

for a living. You smile and say, "I deposit checks."

This is not the life of most authors. But if you follow the advice laid out in this book with passion, and assemble the right strengths on your team, you can get there.

IN AN AGE WHEN THE FASTEST WAY TO BECOME A MILLIONAIRE IS TO START WITH A BILLION DOLLARS,

YOU CAN STILL CREATE THE LIFE YOU WANT.

Go back and look at your Author Score. If it's low, retake it now that you have read and thought about the information in this book. Go to THEBOOKITCH.COM.

If it's high, you're motivated, and it's time to take the next step.

First, be sure you can answer the following questions. If you're not sure, review the chapter listed right after the question.

- Do you have something to say; a legacy worth leaving? (Chapter 1)

- Is it different enough to get you noticed? (Chapter 2)

- Are you passionate enough about it, for it to keep you going? (Chapter 3)

- Can you put together a team that leverages your strengths and builds your business? (Chapter 4-7)

- Will you market well
  enough to make it all
  worthwhile? (Chapter 8)

If you answered *yes* five times, congratulations. There is a book in you. You have the itch. You can scratch. And it will be worth your while to do it.

AUTHOR SCORE QUIZ

FIND OUT IF THERE'S A BOOK INSIDE OF YOU.

Could YOU become a published author? The Author Score is a free, 3-minute quiz that quickly tells if you "have what it takes" to be an author. The 22-question quiz reliably assesses your motivation and readiness to be an author.

Itchless, Scratchy
(LOW MOTIVATION, HIGH READINESS)

You may start with a high degree of clarity and purpose, but like many would-be authors you may give up before you finish and never make your mark.

Itchless, Scratchless
(LOW MOTIVATION, LOW READINESS)

If you start a book project now, you may be wasting your time.

Itchy, Scratchy

(HIGH MOTIVATION, HIGH READINESS)

You can do very well making your mark with a book. Not only can the value you provide take you beyond a book into products and services, but you can get through the ups and downs that it takes to get through to the completion of a book.

Itchy, Scratchless

(HIGH MOTIVATION, LOW READINESS)

If you start a book project now, you can get it done, but you may be in for more time and effort than you thought to make your mark.

TAKE THE QUIZ:
THEBOOKITCH.COM

ADAM D. WITTY

Adam Witty is the Founder and Chief Executive Officer of Advantage Media Group, a publisher of business, self-improvement, and professional development books and online learning. Adam has worked with hundreds of entrepreneurs, business leaders, and professionals to help them share their Stories, Passion, and Knowledge with others through the form of a published book.

Adam is an in-demand speaker and consultant on marketing and business development techniques for entrepreneurs and authors. Adam is the author of *21 Ways to Build Your Business with a Book*. Adam has been featured in *The Wall Street Journal*, *Investors Business Daily*, *Fortune* magazine, and on ABC and Fox and was named to the 2011 *Inc.* magazine 30 Under 30 list of "America's coolest entrepreneurs." In 2012, Adam was selected by the Chilean government to judge the prestigious Start-up Chile! Entrepreneurship competition.

Adam loves to hear from readers. To connect::

> Adam Witty
> c/o Advantage Media Group
> 65 Gadsden Street
> Charleston, SC 29401
> awitty@advantageww.com
> 1.866.755.1696

ALLEN FAHDEN

Author, corporate trainer, and former stand-up comic Allen Fahden has consulted with many Fortune 500 companies, as well as celebrity business owners Paul McCartney and Bill Murray. Allen has been featured by *People* magazine, ABC News, BBC TV, and countless television and radio broadcasts, as well as syndicated and local print media across the US.

Creator of the 1 million selling Team Dimensions Profile, Allen has written chapters for best-selling *The One Minute Millionaire* by *Chicken Soup for the Soul* co-author Mark Victor Hansen. He has also authored *Innovation On Demand* and *Is Half the World Crazy?*

Allen's techniques are a result of years spent developing ways to create new ideas that will sell to both clients and the mass market. His experience in the field includes presiding over his own award-winning advertising agency, as well as serving as Senior Vice-President and Creative Director of D'Arcy, Masius, Benton, and Bowles, and as Senior Writer for accounts such as Levi's at Foote, Cone, and Belding in San Francisco.

Over 30 years working with teams as corporate executive and as a trainer in Edwards Deming's Quality processes, Allen identified an understanding of people's strengths that allows them to triple their performance in the beginning creating, planning and decision stages. By appreciating what a team member can do, and not expecting them to do what they can't, he has freed people to transform their work, relationships and purpose.

REGISTER
YOUR BOOK

AND ACCESS FREE RESOURCES FOR POTENTIAL AUTHORS!

It doesn't matter where you are in the world, Adam and Al can help you share your Stories, Passion, and Knowledge with the world in the form of a published book.

Visit THEBOOKITCH.COM to access these free resources:

 REQUEST a complimentary copy of Adam Witty's best-selling book *21 Ways to Build Your Business with a Book: Secrets to Dramatically Grow Your Income, Credibility, and Celebrity-Power by Being an Author* while supplies last

 RECEIVE a subscription to the Author Success University™ and Insights with Experts™ monthly teleseminars wherein successful authors and book marketing experts reveal their tips and tricks for marketing and growing a business with a book

 REGISTER for a webinar led by Adam Witty: "How to Quickly Write, Publish, And Profit From A Book That Will Explode Your Business"

 COMPLETE Advantage's Publishing Questionnaire and receive a complimentary Discovery Call with an acquisitions editor to help you determine if your ideas, concepts, or manuscript are worth turning into a book

---

ACCESS ALL OF THE ABOVE FREE RESOURCES
BY REGISTERING YOUR BOOK AT
THEBOOKITCH.COM/REGISTER